Kid's Journal: A 5-Year Journaling Workbook with One Question a Day

By KoCo Bean

DEDICATION

This journal is dedicated to kids between 5-11 years old.

Kid's Journal: A 5-Year Journaling Workbook with One Question a Day is perfect for children ages 5 – 11 years old. Not only can they keep a log of all the wonderful things that go on in their ever-changing worlds, but they can improve their writing skills and learn the art of self-reflection.

With daily questions targeted specifically for them and their often busy lives, this kid's writing journal is the perfect companion to get them through their day. Fun daily questions inside a beautifully designed book that they can fill with their personal thoughts, opinions and ideas is the ideal gift for your child and a safe place to keep track of all the monumental events in their young lives.

ACKNOWLEDGMENTS

I would like to thank Coey, GaGa, Mookie, Bob, Spisiak, & Scooby for all their love and support.

January 1st
Make up three New Year's Resolutions.

20__:

20__:

20__:

20__:

20__:

January 2nd
What would you like to learn more about?

20__:

20__:

20__:

20__:

20__:

January 3rd
If you could have any super power, what would it be?

20__:

20__:

20__:

20__:

20__:

January 4th
What do you like the most about January?

20__:

20__:

20__:

20__:

20__:

January 5th
What is the most important thing you've learned in school?

20__:

20__:

20__:

20__:

20__:

January 6th
What are your favorite types of insects?

20__:

20__:

20__:

20__:

20__:

January 7th
What is your favorite season – summer, winter, spring, or fall? Why?

20__:

20__:

20__:

20__:

20__:

January 8th
What do you use computers for?

20__:

20__:

20__:

20__:

20__:

January 9th
Name your favorite character in a book.

20__:

20__:

20__:

20__:

20__:

What are three things you're good at?

20__:

20__:

20__:

20__:

20__:

Which one of your toys would you like to donate to charity?

20__:

20__:

20__:

20__:

20__:

January 12th
Do you think a gorilla would make a good pet? Explain why or why not.

20__:

20__:

20__:

20__:

20__:

January 13th
What is something that makes you unique from everyone else?

20__:

20__:

20__:

20__:

20__:

January 14th
What cheers you up when you're feeling sad?

20__:

20__:

20__:

20__:

20__:

January 15th
If your pet could talk, what would it say?

20__:

20__:

20__:

20__:

20__:

January 16th
Who is your hero?

20__:

20__:

20__:

20__:

20__:

January 17th
What have you learned from your father?

20__:

20__:

20__:

20__:

20__:

January 18th
How would you spend the day if you were invisible?

20__:

20__:

20__:

20__:

20__:

January 19th
What would you do with $1 million dollars?

20__:

20__:

20__:

20__:

20__:

January 20th
What is your favorite outfit to wear?

20__:

20__:

20__:

20__:

20__:

January 21st
What is your favorite Crayon color?

20__:

20__:

20__:

20__:

20__:

January 22nd
What are you thankful for?

20__:

20__:

20__:

20__:

20__:

What is your favorite game to play alone?

20__:

20__:

20__:

20__:

20__:

January 24th
What is the best thing to do on a rainy day?

20__:

20__:

20__:

20__:

20__:

January 25th
What makes you smile?

20__:

20__:

20__:

20__:

20__:

January 26th
What is the funniest joke you've ever heard?

20__:

20__:

20__:

20__:

20__:

January 27th
If you joined the circus, would you be a clown or an acrobat?

20__:

20__:

20__:

20__:

20__:

January 28th
What is your most prized possession?

20__:

20__:

20__:

20__:

20__:

January 29th
What is your favorite thing to do when you're bored?

20__:

20__:

20__:

20__:

20__:

January 30th
If you won an award, what achievement would it most likely be for?

20__:

20__:

20__:

20__:

20__:

January 31st
What is the best thing about being you?

20__:

20__:

20__:

20__:

20__:

February 1st
What do you love the most about your parents?

20__:

20__:

20__:

20__:

20__:

February 2nd
Write down something one of your grandparents told you.

20__:

20__:

20__:

20__:

20__:

February 3rd
Write five words that describe your personality.

20__:

20__:

20__:

20__:

20__:

What does your bedroom look like? Is it messy or clean?

20__:

20__:

20__:

20__:

20__:

February 5th
Describe your best friend.

20__:

20__:

20__:

20__:

20__:

February 6th
Do you get an allowance? If so, what do you spend it on?

20__:

20__:

20__:

20__:

20__:

February 7th
Think as far back in time as you can. What is your very first memory?

20__:

20__:

20__:

20__:

20__:

February 8th
How do you make people laugh?

20__:

20__:

20__:

20__:

20__:

February 9th
Do you exercise regularly? What do you do?

20__:

20__:

20__:

20__:

20__:

February 10th
Do you have straight or curly hair?

20__:

20__:

20__:

20__:

20__:

February 11th
If you wrote a book, what would it be about?

20__:

20__:

20__:

20__:

20__:

February 12th
What is your favorite toy? What is your second favorite?

20__:

20__:

20__:

20__:

20__:

February 13th
What do you love the most about each member of your family?

20__:

20__:

20__:

20__:

20__:

February 14th
List five different objects that are red.

20__:

20__:

20__:

20__:

20__:

February 15th
Do you have any siblings? List them.

20__:

20__:

20__:

20__:

20__:

February 16th
If you could live anywhere in the world, where would you live?

20__:

20__:

20__:

20__:

20__:

February 17th
What do you like about school? What is your favorite activity there?

20__:

20__:

20__:

20__:

20__:

February 18th
What did you eat for breakfast this morning?

20__:

20__:

20__:

20__:

20__:

February 19th
If you got to be the teacher of your classroom for the day, what would you do?

20__:

20__:

20__:

20__:

20__:

February 20th
What is the most exciting thing you've learned this month?

20__:

20__:

20__:

20__:

20__:

February 21st
List three things you can do when you're feeling bored.

20__:

20__:

20__:

20__:

20__:

February 22nd
Describe what you'd like to do at your next birthday party.

20__:

20__:

20__:

20__:

20__:

February 23rd
Would you rather have three eyes or two noses?

20__:

20__:

20__:

20__:

20__:

February 24th
Is it important to have good manners? Do you say Please & Thank you?

20__:

20__:

20__:

20__:

20__:

February 25th
List three things that always make you happy.

20__:

20__:

20__:

20__:

20__:

February 26th
Write three reasons why it's important to be kind to animals.

20__:

20__:

20__:

20__:

20__:

February 27th
Do you know how to write in cursive?

20__:

20__:

20__:

20__:

20__:

February 28th
What is your favorite topping for pizza?

20__:

20__:

20__:

20__:

20__:

March 1st
What is your favorite sound?

20__:

20__:

20__:

20__:

20__:

March 2nd
If you could speak a second language, what language would you speak?

20__:

20__:

20__:

20__:

20__:

March 3rd
What are three things you're good at?

20__:

20__:

20__:

20__:

20__:

March 4th
What is the last thing you got in trouble for?

20__:

20__:

20__:

20__:

20__:

March 5th
What do you like the most about March?

20__:

20__:

20__:

20__:

20__:

March 6th
What are your favorite things to carry around in a backpack?

20__:

20__:

20__:

20__:

20__:

March 7th
Do you have a good luck charm?

20__:

20__:

20__:

20__:

20__:

March 8th
List five different objects that are green.

20__:

20__:

20__:

20__:

20__:

March 9th
List ten things you love about yourself.

20__:

20__:

20__:

20__:

20__:

March 10th
What is the bravest thing you've ever done?

20__:

20__:

20__:

20__:

20__:

Could you live without electricity for one year?

20__:

20__:

20__:

20__:

20__:

March 12th
Who do you trust more than anyone else?

20__:

20__:

20__:

20__:

20__:

What is something you'd like to invent?

20__:

20__:

20__:

20__:

20__:

March 14th
What is the temperature outside today? What time is it?

20__:

20__:

20__:

20__:

20__:

March 15th
Would you rather live in the city or the country?

20__:

20__:

20__:

20__:

20__:

March 16th
What is your lucky number?

20__:

20__:

20__:

20__:

20__:

March 17th
What would you do if you found a pot of gold?

20__:

20__:

20__:

20__:

20__:

March 18th
What does the word empathy mean to you?

20__:

20__:

20__:

20__:

20__:

March 19th
Describe your house.

20__:

20__:

20__:

20__:

20__:

March 20th
What is important to you?

20__:

20__:

20__:

20__:

20__:

March 21st
What did you do for fun this week?

20__:

20__:

20__:

20__:

20__:

Do you have a secret that no one else knows about?

20__:

20__:

20__:

20__:

20__:

March 23rd
What is your favorite hobby?

20__:

20__:

20__:

20__:

20__:

March 24th
What would you do if you were the last person on earth?

20__:

20__:

20__:

20__:

20__:

March 25th
What is something you're really good at?

20__:

20__:

20__:

20__:

20__:

March 26th
What do you like the most about being a kid?

20__:

20__:

20__:

20__:

20__:

March 27th
Describe a beautiful rainbow.

20__:

20__:

20__:

20__:

20__:

March 28th
Do you feel lucky?

20__:

20__:

20__:

20__:

20__:

March 29th
What would you do if you found $20 on the sidewalk?

20__:

20__:

20__:

20__:

20__:

March 30th
What is the best lesson your parents taught you?

20__:

20__:

20__:

20__:

20__:

March 31st
What is your favorite dessert?

20__:

20__:

20__:

20__:

20__:

April 1st
Have you ever played a trick on anyone?

20__:

20__:

20__:

20__:

20__:

April 2nd
What is the meaning of your name? Do you like it?

20__:

20__:

20__:

20__:

20__:

April 3rd
What age would you most like to be? Why?

20__:

20__:

20__:

20__:

20__:

April 4th
What do you like the most about April?

20__:

20__:

20__:

20__:

20__:

April 5th
What important lesson has your mother taught you?

20__:

20__:

20__:

20__:

20__:

April 6th
What charity would you like to volunteer your services at?

20__:

20__:

20__:

20__:

20__:

April 7th
What is your favorite story?

20__:

20__:

20__:

20__:

20__:

April 8th
If you were planting a vegetable garden, what kinds of vegetables would you grow?

20__:

20__:

20__:

20__:

20__:

April 9th
Would you rather play inside or outside?

20__:

20__:

20__:

20__:

20__:

April 10th
What is the grossest thing you've ever seen?

20__:

20__:

20__:

20__:

20__:

April 11th
Which type of physical activity do you prefer – stretching or walking?

20__:

20__:

20__:

20__:

20__:

April 12th
How does your family have fun together?

20__:

20__:

20__:

20__:

20__:

April 13th
What is the funniest thing you've ever seen?

20__:

20__:

20__:

20__:

20__:

April 14th
Do you play a musical instrument?

20__:

20__:

20__:

20__:

20__:

April 15th
What do you like about spring?

20__:

20__:

20__:

20__:

20__:

April 16th
If you could create any type of creature, what would it look like?

20__:

20__:

20__:

20__:

20__:

April 17th
Describe the colors and smells of spring time.

20__:

20__:

20__:

20__:

20__:

April 18th
What is your favorite person from history?

20__:

20__:

20__:

20__:

20__:

April 19th
List three ways you can be a good friend.

20__:

20__:

20__:

20__:

20__:

April 20th
If you could have three wishes what would they be?

20__:

20__:

20__:

20__:

20__:

April 21st
Describe your mom.

20__:

20__:

20__:

20__:

20__:

April 22nd
What is something that makes you laugh?

20__:

20__:

20__:

20__:

20__:

April 23rd
What do you like to do on the weekends?

20__:

20__:

20__:

20__:

20__:

April 24th
What is your favorite cartoon character?

20__:

20__:

20__:

20__:

20__:

April 25th
List one chore you don't like doing.

20__:

20__:

20__:

20__:

20__:

April 26th
What is something you always wanted to do? Will you do it someday?

20__:

20__:

20__:

20__:

20__:

April 27th
What do your friends like about you the most?

20__:

20__:

20__:

20__:

20__:

April 28th
Do you have any rules you have to follow?

20__:

20__:

20__:

20__:

20__:

April 29th
What would you do if you ruled the world?

20__:

20__:

20__:

20__:

20__:

April 30th
What is your favorite kind of weather?

20__:

20__:

20__:

20__:

20__:

What are you thankful for?
May 1st

20__:

20__:

20__:

20__:

20__:

May 2nd
If you could be any animal, what kind would you be?

20__:

20__:

20__:

20__:

20__:

May 3rd
What is your favorite game to play at recess?

20__:

20__:

20__:

20__:

20__:

May 4th
What do you like the most about May?

20__:

20__:

20__:

20__:

20__:

May 5th
What is your favorite food?

20__:

20__:

20__:

20__:

20__:

May 6th
What would be a good nickname for you?

20__:

20__:

20__:

20__:

20__:

Some people collect stamps or coins. Do you collect anything?

20__:

20__:

20__:

20__:

20__:

May 8th
What is your favorite vegetable?

20__:

20__:

20__:

20__:

20__:

May 9th
List some ways you can help other people.

20__:

20__:

20__:

20__:

20__:

<u>May 10th</u>
How do you cheer yourself up when you're having a bad day?

20__:

20__:

20__:

20__:

20__:

May 11th
What is your favorite book?

20__:

20__:

20__:

20__:

20__:

May 12th
If you could go anywhere, where would you go?

20__:

20__:

20__:

20__:

20__:

May 13th
List three things you want to do today.

20__:

20__:

20__:

20__:

20__:

May 14th
Who is your favorite teacher?

20__:

20__:

20__:

20__:

20__:

May 15th
What is your favorite song?

20__:

20__:

20__:

20__:

20__:

May 16th
Describe your Dad.

20__:

20__:

20__:

20__:

20__:

May 17th
Describe your last dream.

20__:

20__:

20__:

20__:

20__:

May 18th
If you could change places with anyone, who would it be?

20__:

20__:

20__:

20__:

20__:

May 19th
Do you have brothers or sisters?

20__:

20__:

20__:

20__:

20__:

May 20th
Do you remember getting your hair cut for the first time?

20__:

20__:

20__:

20__:

20__:

What are your three favorite foods?

20__:

20__:

20__:

20__:

20__:

May 22nd
Where do you want to go for your next vacation?

20__:

20__:

20__:

20__:

20__:

May 23rd
Describe one time you stayed up late. What did you do?

20__:

20__:

20__:

20__:

20__:

May 24th
If you could travel back in time, where would you go?

20__:

20__:

20__:

20__:

20__:

Would you rather have $1000 to spend on yourself or $10,000 to give away?

20__:

20__:

20__:

20__:

20__:

May 26th
What would you like to do when you're grown up?

20__:

20__:

20__:

20__:

20__:

May 27th
What is the nicest compliment anyone has given you?

20__:

20__:

20__:

20__:

20__:

May 28th
What is something you like shopping for?

20__:

20__:

20__:

20__:

20__:

May 29th
What is the best birthday present you've ever received?

20__:

20__:

20__:

20__:

20__:

May 30th
If you could eat only one kind of food for a week, what would it be?

20__:

20__:

20__:

20__:

20__:

May 31st
What do you like most about school?

20__:

20__:

20__:

20__:

20__:

June 1st
What do you like about summer?

20__:

20__:

20__:

20__:

20__:

June 2nd
What is the coolest place you've ever visited?

20__:

20__:

20__:

20__:

20__:

June 3rd
If someone gave you $500 to spend, what would you buy?

20__:

20__:

20__:

20__:

20__:

June 4th
When is the last time you made a mistake?

20__:

20__:

20__:

20__:

20__:

June 5th
What was the happiest day in your life?

20__:

20__:

20__:

20__:

20__:

June 6th
What do you like the most about June?

20__:

20__:

20__:

20__:

20__:

June 7th
Is there a famous person you would like to meet?

20__:

20__:

20__:

20__:

20__:

June 8th
What would you do if you were a butterfly?

20__:

20__:

20__:

20__:

20__:

June 9th
Is there something you can do really well?

20__:

20__:

20__:

20__:

20__:

June 10th
What is your favorite type of music?

20__:

20__:

20__:

20__:

20__:

June 11th
How do you like to spend your free time?

20__:

20__:

20__:

20__:

20__:

June 12th
What qualities do you look for in a friend?

20__:

20__:

20__:

20__:

20__:

June 13th
What would you like to do today?

20__:

20__:

20__:

20__:

20__:

June 14th
If you could pick a new name for yourself, what would it be?

20__:

20__:

20__:

20__:

20__:

June 15th
List five different objects that are yellow.

20__:

20__:

20__:

20__:

20__:

June 16th
What is your favorite type of flower?

20__:

20__:

20__:

20__:

20__:

June 17th
What is your first memory?

20__:

20__:

20__:

20__:

20__:

June 18th
What is your favorite day of the week?

20__:

20__:

20__:

20__:

20__:

June 19th
What would you do if your electricity went out for the day?

20__:

20__:

20__:

20__:

20__:

June 20th
What movie character would you like to meet?

20__:

20__:

20__:

20__:

20__:

June 21st
What are you planning to do today?

20__:

20__:

20__:

20__:

20__:

June 22nd
What is the best lesson your grandparents taught you?

20__:

20__:

20__:

20__:

20__:

<u>June 23rd</u>
Describe the last time you felt embarrassed.

20__:

20__:

20__:

20__:

20__:

June 24th
If you were only one inch tall how would your life be different?

20__:

20__:

20__:

20__:

20__:

June 25th
What books do you want to read?

20__:

20__:

20__:

20__:

20__:

June 26th
If you had to go live on a deserted island, what would you bring?

20__:

20__:

20__:

20__:

20__:

June 27th
Who is someone that you admire?

20__:

20__:

20__:

20__:

20__:

June 28th
What is something you are grateful for?

20__:

20__:

20__:

20__:

20__:

June 29th
List the people that you love.

20__:

20__:

20__:

20__:

20__:

June 30th
What do you like to do for fun?

20__:

20__:

20__:

20__:

20__:

<u>July 1st</u>
What are the characteristics of a hero?

20__:

20__:

20__:

20__:

20__:

July 2nd
What kind of food would you bring to a picnic?

20__:

20__:

20__:

20__:

20__:

July 3rd
If you could talk to any person that ever lived in history, who & what would you say?

20__:

20__:

20__:

20__:

20__:

July 4th
What makes you most proud?

20__:

20__:

20__:

20__:

20__:

July 5th
What song do you like to sing out loud? Please sing it.

20__:

20__:

20__:

20__:

20__:

July 6th
What do you like the most about July?

20__:

20__:

20__:

20__:

20__:

July 7th
What is your favorite outdoor game?

20__:

20__:

20__:

20__:

20__:

July 8th
Would you like to be able to talk to animals?

20__:

20__:

20__:

20__:

20__:

July 9th
What is your favorite type of weather?

20__:

20__:

20__:

20__:

20__:

July 10th
What types of animals would you most like to visit at the zoo?

20__:

20__:

20__:

20__:

20__:

July 11th
If you wrote a short story, what would it be about?

20__:

20__:

20__:

20__:

20__:

July 12th
If you owned a store, what type of products would you sell?

20__:

20__:

20__:

20__:

20__:

July 13th
Would you like to be old or young?

20__:

20__:

20__:

20__:

20__:

July 14th
What is the strangest thing you have ever seen?

20__:

20__:

20__:

20__:

20__:

July 15th
What is your favorite junk food?

20__:

20__:

20__:

20__:

20__:

July 16th
Describe your most recent dream.

20__:

20__:

20__:

20__:

20__:

July 17th
Would you rather be hot or cold?

20__:

20__:

20__:

20__:

20__:

July 18th
What would you do if you couldn't watch television for a week?

20__:

20__:

20__:

20__:

20__:

July 19th
If you had one wish what would it be?

20__:

20__:

20__:

20__:

20__:

July 20th
What is your favorite kind of ice cream?

20__:

20__:

20__:

20__:

20__:

July 21st
Is your room tidy or sloppy?

20__:

20__:

20__:

20__:

20__:

July 22nd
List five different objects that are blue.

20__:

20__:

20__:

20__:

20__:

July 23rd
What if you were able to fly, where would you go?

20__:

20__:

20__:

20__:

20__:

July 24th
What do you like the most about yourself?

20__:

20__:

20__:

20__:

20__:

July 25th
What award would you like to win?

20__:

20__:

20__:

20__:

20__:

July 26th
What hair color would you like to have?

20__:

20__:

20__:

20__:

20__:

July 27th
Look up at the sky and describe what it looks like.

20__:

20__:

20__:

20__:

20__:

July 28th
What is your favorite thing to do on a hot day?

20__:

20__:

20__:

20__:

20__:

July 29th
What is the bravest thing you've ever done?

20__:

20__:

20__:

20__:

20__:

July 30th
Where would you like to go for a summer vacation?

20__:

20__:

20__:

20__:

20__:

July 31st
Have you ever gotten into a water balloon fight? Do you want to?

20__:

20__:

20__:

20__:

20__:

August 1st
Make up a brand new holiday.

20__:

20__:

20__:

20__:

20__:

Which one of your many talents would you display, if you performed at a talent show?

20__:

20__:

20__:

20__:

20__:

August 3rd
Do you feel best in the morning, afternoon, or evening?

20__:

20__:

20__:

20__:

20__:

August 4th
What do you like the most about August?

20__:

20__:

20__:

20__:

20__:

August 5th
What places have you traveled to?

20__:

20__:

20__:

20__:

20__:

August 6th
What would be the perfect day for you?

20__:

20__:

20__:

20__:

20__:

August 7th
If you could make any slogan for a t-shirt, what would it be?

20__:

20__:

20__:

20__:

20__:

August 8th
Name three things that are beautiful.

20__:

20__:

20__:

20__:

20__:

August 9th
What is your favorite season?

20__:

20__:

20__:

20__:

20__:

August 10th
Who are your favorite cartoon characters?

20__:

20__:

20__:

20__:

20__:

August 11th
What is a place that you would like to visit?

20__:

20__:

20__:

20__:

20__:

August 12th
Who do you think is the most interesting person in history?

20__:

20__:

20__:

20__:

20__:

August 13th
If you could choose any musical instrument to play, what would it be?

20__:

20__:

20__:

20__:

20__:

August 14th
Imagine if you were president for the day. What would you do?

20__:

20__:

20__:

20__:

20__:

August 15th
What do you think is the most important rule?

20__:

20__:

20__:

20__:

20__:

August 16th
What is your favorite hobby?

20__:

20__:

20__:

20__:

20__:

Is there something that really bothers you?

20__:

20__:

20__:

20__:

20__:

August 18th
How do you help around the house?

20__:

20__:

20__:

20__:

20__:

August 19th
What is the best thing about unicorns?

20__:

20__:

20__:

20__:

20__:

August 20th
Do you prefer to listen to music, play games, read books, or watch movies?

20__:

20__:

20__:

20__:

20__:

August 21st
Who do you talk to when you have a problem?

20__:

20__:

20__:

20__:

20__:

August 22nd
Have you ever flown on an airplane?

20__:

20__:

20__:

20__:

20__:

August 23rd
Would you prefer to live in the past, present, or future?

20__:

20__:

20__:

20__:

20__:

August 24th
What is your favorite type of animal?

20__:

20__:

20__:

20__:

20__:

August 25th
What is the most exciting thing that happened this week?

20__:

20__:

20__:

20__:

20__:

August 26th
What do you like about the beach?

20__:

20__:

20__:

20__:

20__:

August 27th
Pretend that you just invented a brand new toy. Please describe it.

20__:

20__:

20__:

20__:

20__:

August 28th
Why is honesty important?

20__:

20__:

20__:

20__:

20__:

August 29th
If you had a camera, what would you take pictures of?

20__:

20__:

20__:

20__:

20__:

August 30th
What do you think the world will be like 20 years from now?

20__:

20__:

20__:

20__:

20__:

August 31st
Make a list of three things that you could teach to others.

20__:

20__:

20__:

20__:

20__:

<u>September 1st</u>
What I know about dogs is that...

20__:

20__:

20__:

20__:

20__:

September 2nd
If I were granted three wishes what would they be and why?

20__:

20__:

20__:

20__:

20__:

September 3rd
When is the last time you broke a rule?

20__:

20__:

20__:

20__:

20__:

September 4th
If you could fly wherever you wanted to, where would you go?

20__:

20__:

20__:

20__:

20__:

September 5th
What is it like on the first day of school?

20__:

20__:

20__:

20__:

20__:

September 6th
If you could be on any TV show, which one would you choose?

20__:

20__:

20__:

20__:

20__:

September 7th
What was the scariest experience in your entire life?

20__:

20__:

20__:

20__:

20__:

September 8th
What do you like the most about September?

20__:

20__:

20__:

20__:

20__:

September 9th
Is there anything you would like to change about yourself?

20__:

20__:

20__:

20__:

20__:

September 10th
How many teeth do you have?

20__:

20__:

20__:

20__:

20__:

September 11th
What would be the best day for flying a kite?

20__:

20__:

20__:

20__:

20__:

September 12th
What is your favorite color?

20__:

20__:

20__:

20__:

20__:

September 13th
How would you react if someone was bullying you?

20__:

20__:

20__:

20__:

20__:

September 14th
Who is the oldest person you know?

20__:

20__:

20__:

20__:

20__:

September 15th
List three ways you can show your appreciation for your Mom or Dad.

20__:

20__:

20__:

20__:

20__:

September 16th
How do you show people that you care about them?

20__:

20__:

20__:

20__:

20__:

September 17th
How would you like to decorate your bedroom?

20__:

20__:

20__:

20__:

20__:

September 18th
Describe a thunderstorm.

20__:

20__:

20__:

20__:

20__:

September 19th
Make up a headline for a newspaper article.

20__:

20__:

20__:

20__:

20__:

September 20th
What is the coziest spot in your home?

20__:

20__:

20__:

20__:

20__:

September 21st
If you started your own business, what would you do?

20__:

20__:

20__:

20__:

20__:

September 22nd
Do you know how to make a paper airplane?

20__:

20__:

20__:

20__:

20__:

September 23rd
Imagine you're a dinosaur. What would you do all day?

20__:

20__:

20__:

20__:

20__:

September 24th
If you could have a classroom pet, what kind of animal would you choose?

20__:

20__:

20__:

20__:

20__:

September 25th
What kind of creatures live in the ocean?

20__:

20__:

20__:

20__:

20__:

September 26th
List three superheroes.

20__:

20__:

20__:

20__:

20__:

September 27th
I am special because...

20__:

20__:

20__:

20__:

20__:

September 28th
What kind of animals live in the woods?

20__:

20__:

20__:

20__:

20__:

September 29th
What would you do if there was no Internet or phones for a month?

20__:

20__:

20__:

20__:

20__:

September 30th
List some fun indoor activities.

20__:

20__:

20__:

20__:

20__:

October 1st
What is your favorite subject in school?

20__:

20__:

20__:

20__:

20__:

October 2nd
What do you like the most about October?

20__:

20__:

20__:

20__:

20__:

October 3rd
If you could tell your friends one thing, what would it be?

20__:

20__:

20__:

20__:

20__:

October 4th
Who is your favorite teacher?

20__:

20__:

20__:

20__:

20__:

October 5th
What would you bring to show and tell?

20__:

20__:

20__:

20__:

20__:

October 6th
When is the last time someone helped you?

20__:

20__:

20__:

20__:

20__:

October 7th
Who is the youngest person you know?

20__:

20__:

20__:

20__:

20__:

October 8th
Have you ever argued with anyone?

20__:

20__:

20__:

20__:

20__:

October 9th
Make a list of three things you learned in the last week.

20__:

20__:

20__:

20__:

20__:

<u>October 10th</u>
What sort of meals should be served in a school cafeteria?

20__:

20__:

20__:

20__:

20__:

October 11th
Do you think that school children should be given homework?

20__:

20__:

20__:

20__:

20__:

October 12th
What would you like to change about your school?

20__:

20__:

20__:

20__:

20__:

October 13th
What is the most disgusting smell?

20__:

20__:

20__:

20__:

20__:

October 14th
If you could have three wishes granted, what would they be?

20__:

20__:

20__:

20__:

20__:

October 15th
If you could meet any person, who would it be?

20__:

20__:

20__:

20__:

20__:

October 16th
What do you wish other people knew about you?

20__:

20__:

20__:

20__:

20__:

October 17th
Write a joke here.

20__:

20__:

20__:

20__:

20__:

October 18th
What are three fun places to visit?

20__:

20__:

20__:

20__:

20__:

October 19th
What do your friends like about you?

20__:

20__:

20__:

20__:

20__:

October 20th
Would you prefer to travel in a car, train, or plane?

20__:

20__:

20__:

20__:

20__:

October 21st
How will you become famous one day?

20__:

20__:

20__:

20__:

20__:

October 22nd
What do you like best about your neighborhood?

20__:

20__:

20__:

20__:

20__:

October 23rd
If you go on a trip for the weekend, what three things would you bring?

20__:

20__:

20__:

20__:

20__:

October 24th
How can you help others?

20__:

20__:

20__:

20__:

20__:

October 25th
I'd like to invent a machine that would...

20__:

20__:

20__:

20__:

20__:

October 26th
What is the biggest thing you ever saw?

20__:

20__:

20__:

20__:

20__:

October 27th
Do you have any bad habits?

20__:

20__:

20__:

20__:

20__:

October 28th
What rule would you like to create and have everyone follow?

20__:

20__:

20__:

20__:

20__:

October 29th
Do you have a favorite quote?

20__:

20__:

20__:

20__:

20__:

If you won $1 million how would you spend it?

20__:

20__:

20__:

20__:

20__:

October 31st
Do you have a haunted house in your area?

20__:

20__:

20__:

20__:

20__:

November 1st
What do you like the most about November?

20__:

20__:

20__:

20__:

20__:

November 2nd
Do you like hot cocoa with marshmallows?

20__:

20__:

20__:

20__:

20__:

November 3rd
Describe a snowflake.

20__:

20__:

20__:

20__:

20__:

November 4th
Describe your favorite holiday decorations.

20__:

20__:

20__:

20__:

20__:

November 5th
What are five things you would like to do this winter?

20__:

20__:

20__:

20__:

20__:

November 6th
What is the temperature outside right now?

20__:

20__:

20__:

20__:

20__:

November 7th
What are three things you can do to become a better student?

20__:

20__:

20__:

20__:

20__:

November 8th
If you could change one thing what would it be?

20__:

20__:

20__:

20__:

20__:

November 9th
What is something you would never do?

20__:

20__:

20__:

20__:

20__:

November 10th
What age would you like to be?

20__:

20__:

20__:

20__:

20__:

November 11th
What is your favorite food to eat for lunch?

20__:

20__:

20__:

20__:

20__:

November 12th
What would you do if you could stop time?

20__:

20__:

20__:

20__:

20__:

November 13th
What made you smile today?

20__:

20__:

20__:

20__:

20__:

November 14th
What are you grateful for?

20__:

20__:

20__:

20__:

20__:

November 15th
If you could change your name what would it be?

20__:

20__:

20__:

20__:

20__:

November 16th
What do you enjoy doing with your family?

20__:

20__:

20__:

20__:

20__:

November 17th
What is one thing you're excited about?

20__:

20__:

20__:

20__:

20__:

November 18th
What is your favorite family tradition?

20__:

20__:

20__:

20__:

20__:

November 19th
What is the single most important quality in a person?

20__:

20__:

20__:

20__:

20__:

If you could have an unlimited supply of one thing, what would it be?

20__:

20__:

20__:

20__:

20__:

November 21st
How would you improve the world?

20__:

20__:

20__:

20__:

20__:

November 22nd
What made you happy today?

20__:

20__:

20__:

20__:

20__:

November 23rd
What is your definition of love?

20__:

20__:

20__:

20__:

20__:

November 24th
How do you take care of someone that is sick?

20__:

20__:

20__:

20__:

20__:

November 25th
What is something you don't understand?

20__:

20__:

20__:

20__:

20__:

November 26th
I am thankful for...

20__:

20__:

20__:

20__:

20__:

November 27th
When is the last time you cried?

20__:

20__:

20__:

20__:

20__:

November 28th
What do you know about stars?

20__:

20__:

20__:

20__:

20__:

November 29th
What did you learn today?

20__:

20__:

20__:

20__:

20__:

November 30th
What is your favorite movie and why?

20__:

20__:

20__:

20__:

20__:

December 1st
What do you like the most about December?

20__:

20__:

20__:

20__:

20__:

December 2nd
Have you ever played in the snow?

20__:

20__:

20__:

20__:

20__:

December 3rd
What kind of gift can you make that doesn't cost anything?

20__:

20__:

20__:

20__:

20__:

December 4th
What is your favorite kind of candy?

20__:

20__:

20__:

20__:

20__:

What is your favorite holiday?

20__:

20__:

20__:

20__:

20__:

December 6th
What is the best gift you've ever received?

20__:

20__:

20__:

20__:

20__:

December 7th
What is your favorite dessert?

20__:

20__:

20__:

20__:

20__:

What would you do if you traded places with your parents for one day?

20__:

20__:

20__:

20__:

20__:

December 9th
Are there any words that you think are funny? List them here.

20__:

20__:

20__:

20__:

20__:

December 10th
What is something you're good at?

20__:

20__:

20__:

20__:

20__:

December 11th
Where did you go today?

20__:

20__:

20__:

20__:

20__:

December 12th
What are five things you like about yourself?

20__:

20__:

20__:

20__:

20__:

December 13th
What do you think about when you're falling asleep?

20__:

20__:

20__:

20__:

20__:

December 14th
Who do you admire the most?

20__:

20__:

20__:

20__:

20__:

December 15th
What is the best thing that happened this month?

20__:

20__:

20__:

20__:

20__:

December 16th
If you could have lunch with anyone in the world who would it be?

20__:

20__:

20__:

20__:

20__:

December 17th
If you could have an unlimited supply of one thing, what would it be?

20__:

20__:

20__:

20__:

20__:

What are ways to have fun without spending any money?

20__:

20__:

20__:

20__:

20__:

December 19th
What is your favorite time of day?

20__:

20__:

20__:

20__:

20__:

December 20th
What is the funniest thing that happened to you today?

20__:

20__:

20__:

20__:

20__:

December 21st
On a scale of one to ten, how happy are you?

20__:

20__:

20__:

20__:

20__:

December 22nd
What are three things you want to learn?

20__:

20__:

20__:

20__:

20__:

December 23rd
What is your favorite time of the year and why?

20__:

20__:

20__:

20__:

20__:

December 24th
Describe your day in five words.

20__:

20__:

20__:

20__:

20__:

December 25th
List the best things that happened today.

20__:

20__:

20__:

20__:

20__:

December 26th
Do you talk to yourself? What do you say?

20__:

20__:

20__:

20__:

20__:

December 27th
If you were a cartoon character, who would you be?

20__:

20__:

20__:

20__:

20__:

December 28th
Look out your window and describe the view.

20__:

20__:

20__:

20__:

20__:

December 29th
What makes you laugh?

20__:

20__:

20__:

20__:

20__:

December 30th
What is your favorite sound?

20__:

20__:

20__:

20__:

20__:

December 31st
What are three things you like about yourself?

20__:

20__:

20__:

20__:

20__:

ABOUT THE AUTHOR

KoCo Bean is a small self-publishing author, creating 5-year questionnaire journals. Each one is a labor of love - created especially for memory keeping, self-discovery and inspiration.

Made in the USA
Columbia, SC
18 December 2021

52023798R00207